Dog Agility

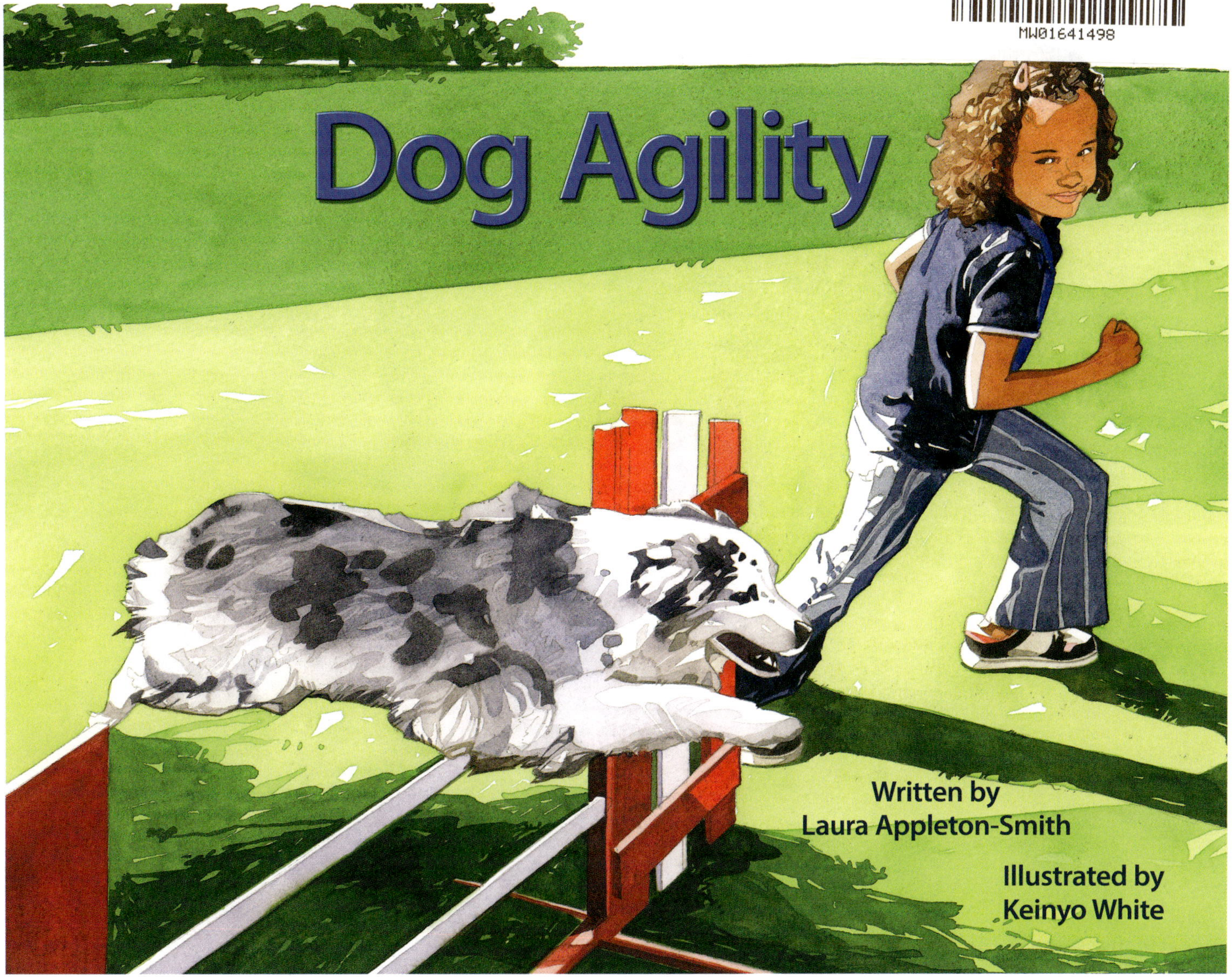

Written by
Laura Appleton-Smith

Illustrated by
Keinyo White

For Norah and Bodie.
LAS

For Ajani and Scarlett.
KW

Laura Appleton-Smith holds a degree in English from Middlebury College. Laura is a primary school teacher who has combined her talents in creative writing with her experience in early childhood education to create *Books to Remember*. She lives in New Hampshire with her husband, Terry.

Keinyo White is a graduate of the Rhode Island School of Design with a B.F.A. in illustration. He currently produces children's books and freelance illustrations from his studio in Los Angeles.

Text copyright © 2011 Laura Appleton-Smith
Illustration copyright © 2007 Keinyo White

All Rights Reserved
No part of this book may be reproduced or transmitted in any form or by any means, electronic, mechanical, photocopying, recording, or otherwise, without prior written permission from the publisher.
For information, contact Flyleaf Publishing.

A Book to Remember™
Published by Flyleaf Publishing

For orders or information, contact us at **(800) 449-7006**.
Please visit our website at **www.flyleafpublishing.com**

Second Edition 6/14
Library of Congress Catalog Card Number: 2008937541
ISBN-13: 978-1-60541-012-8
Printed and bound in the USA at Worzalla Publishing, Stevens Point, WI 6/14

Contents

Chapter 1
Agility Dogs and Handlers

Dog agility is a challenging sport for dogs and their handlers.

In dog agility, dogs must do an obstacle course as fast as they can. An obstacle can be a fence, a ramp, a ring, or a box.

Agility dogs can be
any breed or size.

Dogs that succeed,
or do well, in agility
are fast and intelligent.
They have good balance
and are good jumpers.

Handlers can be kids or adults.

The handler's job is to run next to the dog.
The handler tells the dog which obstacle to go to next.

Chapter 2
The Obstacles

Dog Walk

This obstacle is called a dog walk.

A dog walk looks like a bridge.
The dog must go up the ramp,
cross the flat plank in the center,
and then go back down.

Teeter-Totter

This obstacle is called a teeter-totter.

A plank is set on a hinge.
The dog runs up the plank until it tips.
Then the dog can run back down.

Ring Jump

This obstacle is called a ring jump.

The ring hangs on a stand.
The dog must jump through the ring.

Pause Box

This obstacle is called a pause box.

The dog must get on top of the box and not budge for 5 seconds.

Weave Poles

This obstacle is called weave poles.

The dog must dodge quickly in and out of the poles. This is a challenging obstacle for dogs to master.

Chapter 3
An Excellent Sport

Agility dogs are judged by how fast they are. The fastest dog to finish all of the obstacles on the course wins the contest.

If a dog and its handler are in the top 4 spots in a dog agility contest, they will often win a ribbon.

Dog agility is a fun sport for kids or adults who like dogs.
It is an excellent sport for dogs that are intelligent and fast.

Prerequisite Skills

Single consonants and short vowels
Final double consonants ***ff***, ***gg***, ***ll***, ***nn***, ***ss***, ***tt***, ***zz***
Consonant /k/ ***ck***
Consonant digraphs /ng/ ***ng***, ***n[k]***, /th/ ***th***, /hw/ ***wh***
Schwa /ə/ ***a***, ***e***, ***i***, ***o***, ***u***
Long /ē/ ***ee***, ***y***
r-Controlled /ûr/ ***er***
Variant vowel /aw/ ***al***, ***all***
Consonant /l/ ***le***
/d/ or /t/ ***–ed***

Prerequisite Skills are foundational phonics skills that have been previously introduced.

Target Letter-Sound Correspondence is the letter-sound correspondence introduced in the story.

High-Frequency Puzzle Words are high-frequency irregular words.

Story Puzzle Words are irregular words that are not high frequency.

Decodable Words are words that can be decoded solely on the basis of the letter-sound correspondences or phonetic elements that have been introduced.

Target Letter-Sound Correspondence

Consonant /j/ sound spelled ***g***

agility
hinge
intelligent

Target Letter-Sound Correspondence

Consonant /j/ sound spelled ***dge***

bridge	dodge
budge	judged

Target Letter-Sound Correspondence

Consonant /s/ sound spelled ***c***

balance	fence
center	succeed
excellent	

High-Frequency Puzzle Words

any	looks
are	of
be	often
by	or
do	out
down	their
for	they
go	through
good	to
have	which
how	who
like	

Story Puzzle Words

challenging	poles
chapter	size
course	sport
finish	weave
pause	

Decodable Words

1
2
3
4
5
a
adults
all
an
and
as
back
box
breed
called
can
contest
cross
dog
dogs
fast
fastest
flat
fun
get
handler
handler's
handlers
hangs
if
in
is
it
its
job
jump
jumpers
kids
master
must
next
not
obstacle
obstacles
on
plank
quickly
ramp
ribbon
ring
run
runs
seconds
set
spots
stand
teeter-totter
tells
that
the
then
this
tips
top
until
up
walk
well
will
win
wins